HEARTENING POEMS

HARSHITHA NADIKUDA

This book has been published with all efforts taken to make the material error-free after the consent of the author. However, the author and the publisher do not assume and hereby disclaim any liability to any party for any loss, damage, or disruption caused by errors or omissions, whether such errors or omissions result from negligence, accident, or any other cause.

While every effort has been made to avoid any mistake or omission, this publication is being sold on the condition and understanding that neither the author nor the publishers or printers would be liable in any manner to any person by reason of any mistake or omission in this publication or for any action taken or omitted to be taken or advice rendered or accepted on the basis of this work. For any defect in printing or binding the publishers will be liable only to replace the defective copy by another copy of this work then available.

Contents

Preface

Heartening Poems is a collection of mellifluous poems, penned by poets and poetesses.

Inspiration is an essential ingredient for success in any field. Inspiration awakens us to new possibilities by allowing us to transcend our ordinary experiences and limitations. Inspiration propels a person from apathy to possibility, and transforms the way we perceive our own capabilities. Hence, co-authors aspires to inspire people via mesmerizing verses.

Acknowledgements

I feel a great sense of gratitude towards God for guiding me through his blessings in the whole process of compiling this anthology.
Special thanks to all the co-authors of this book. Without the efforts of co-authors this book wouldn't come into life.
I would like to thank all my well-wishers for supporting me.
And finally, I kindly thank the readers in advance.

1. WAIVE WORRIES

Withholding worries
Will weave weakness,
While wail waddles, witnessing;
Wake, wisdomly welcome ways
Which would wane wobbles.
– Harshitha Nadikuda

ABOUT THE AUTHOR

Harshitha Nadikuda, passionate poetess from Hyderabad, Telangana. She do believe that the words which are penned hold a louder voice, than which are spoken. Hence, she converts her thoughts into writings to have a voice in a world full of noise.

2. ACROSTIC: INSPIRATION

Inspire oneself when low,
Nostalgic being to be in past success.
Success will come to door step,
Prioritise our work first.
Idolize to be a boss,
Resilient in every profit and loss.
Accomplishment of sky,
Try always to fly high.
Interrogate new challenges,
Obstruct all the negativity,
Nurture ourself to be the best.
– Rashmi Kiran

ABOUT THE AUTHOR

Rashmi Kiran is a student. She belongs to Jamshedpur, Jharkhand. Writing is her passion. She loves to transfer the buds of thoughts into roses of words that can blossom at least someone's life. By God's grace, she could write two books completely owned by her "PERSPECTIVE OF SOCIETY" and "A SMALL THOUGHT" from Notion Publication. She has compiled an anthology too "ALEATOIRE" , "BEING

OPTIMISTA" and "ESQUISSER LA PEINTURE" from the same publication house. Presenting her in lot more waves of anthologies. She also has her own podcast channel which ranked 63 in UAE. The name of the podcast channel is "WHAT AUTHOR FEELS". She welcomes creative minds who could bring a positive look to the world.

3. NEVER STOP BEING A GOOD PERSON

Goodness is a pious and precious All can't afford to have this divine virtue, hue.
Evilness always tries to overpower it,
Taint it with its sinister intentions, Sticks to it like an unwanted impurity,
But endeavour to brush it aside.
Let this poisonous air not pollute your mind, Let this abysmal pouring not erode your goodness,
Create an armour around you Made up of endurance, fortitude and gratitude,
Dotted with Ignorance, purity of heart and a congenial smile.
Have you seen river Ganga losing its Divinity?
Despite how human throw their waste with reckless insanity,
Neverthless, it flows in its holiness.
Bad behaviour is manifestation of their demeanor, behaviour.
You should hold onto your true Let it sparkle like a gem amidst the heap of coal.
– Harshita Saha

ABOUT THE AUTHOR

Harshita is 21 years old medical student.

She is from Ranchi, Jharkhand.

She is a writer and has been writing since two years ago.

Also interested in cooking, art and travelling.

You can interact with her on facebook: Sherlien S or : _harsh.ita_6301_.

She has secretly discovered the rule breaking magic of content writing and article making.

4. YOU ARE BRAVE

Despite of all sorts of tension,
You choose to enjoy,
YOU ARE BRAVE!
Despite of all the betrayal getting from universe,
You choose to be trustworthy,
YOU ARE BRAVE!
Despite of being heartbroken,
You choose to be loyal yet,
YOU ARE BRAVE!
Despite of living in this orthodox world,
You choose to be unconventional,
YOU ARE BRAVE!
Despite of being so much reason to be sad,
You choose Happiness,
You choose to stay happy,
"YOU ARE BRAVE"!
– Anjali Jain

ABOUT THE AUTHOR

Anjali Jain loves to understand people and learn from them. A curious writer, her words are sword as well as shield. She

always keeps on hunting for new opportunities & ways of life. You will be getting some amazing and creative content from her mind. She likes to write quotes, poems, research articles, blogs, basically everything as she says 'Bleeding Thoughts'.
Learning & speaking different languages is her favorite task. Perfection in work is the only thing she wants! She quoted, "My hobby keeps on changing with time. Still exploring myself!"
Instagram writer @a.j_moyotales

5. INSPIRATION

Life is an opportunity, benefit from it
Life is beauty, admire it
Life is a dream, relaize it
Life is a challenge, meet it
Life is a duty, complete it
Life is a game, play it
Life is a promise, fulfill it
Life is sorrow, overcome it
Life is a song, sing it
Life is a struggle, accept it
Life is a tragedy, confront it
Life is an adventure, dare it
Life is lucky, Make it
Life is too precious, do not destroy it
Life is Life, fight for it
– Jasmine swetha.M

ABOUT THE AUTHOR

Jasmine swetha.M is from Coimbatore, Tamil Nadu. She's pursuing BBA in Nirmala college for women. Writing is her passion and degree is for her profession. She writes essays, poems and quotes. She has co-authored many anthologies.

6. LOST IN LIFE

You might lose after trying your best
You might mess up for making haste
You might lose yourself in the night
But the sun will guide you by its light
Don't worry, you've not yet lost in life
Darkness may enter in you
Ripping you off your skin.
You might find no way , no hope to win
Don't run away, keep aside that knife
You're safe,you've not yet lost in life
You maybe tender
But your different
You might keep yourself isolated
But you are god-sent
You might lose four but you still have five
You're still the same don't worry
You're not yet lost in life
When evil weakens you
And the chances of victory of truth are very few
When you are striving for your right
Don't be afraid, you've not yet lost in life
When a ray of hope makes its way into the dark
Out of a burnt matchstick

Appears a spark
When the stale part of you lacks strength
Still you want to fight, till your last breath
Carry on; you've not yet lost in life
– Ishita Banerjee

ABOUT THE AUTHOR

Ishita Banerjee was born in January 2003 in kolkata, West Bengal studied till class 12 at St. Pauls boarding and day school, Kolkata. Currently pursuing BBA(Hospital Management) in NSHM Knowledge Campus, Kolkata. She has been writing poems ever since class 6. Some of her works has also have been published in some local newspapers like The Telegraph(TTIS) and school magazines. Her poems have been featured in the book THE LAST FLOWER OF SPRING by Poem Pajama publications under Delhi Poerty Slam. "WHISPER OF HEARTS" by Bookfever publications and " MIRAKEE " by TGIWC. She also wants to write more in future and inspire all the sections of the society.

7. HATS OF TO HANGAL KUMAR SWAMIJI

I surrendered so much in history, great
I have heard about the Great peoples and Cons of the same
I have tried writing about the ascetic here.
I stayed at Badami Shiv Yoga Mandira in Bagalkot district for a month
In those days, I realized the life history of
shree hangal kumar swamiji
Trying to tell as much as I know
Hangal Kumara Shivayogi from his birth
Who worked for society until death
Those who have prolonged society by
all kind of revolution
He lead his life like how great swamijis
should live
The main reason why there are great Swamijis in today's society is all the great efforts
Hangal kumar swamiji
Cows Conservation Monastery, Vibhuti Vigilance Center, For the poor,
Dalits, the poor, the blind,The shelter of rice

Kannada Vachana Literature Collection and
All India Veershayava Mahasabha was
founded
He given alot of Contribution to society
But he never taken name and fame
In Entire History British will not left anyone
Easily But they Given land to Hangal Kumar swamji Because of His all kind of revolution
As long as there is a Sun and moon, Kumar swamji life story inspires
Life inspires
Salute to infinite power of Kumar swamji
- Santhosh v Shirasangi

ABOUT THE AUTHOR

Santhosh V Shirasangi is a student of Psychology, English literature and Journalism

8. THE NATURE

May the sun
Brings us new energy by a new day .
May the moon
Softly restore us by the night .
May the stars
Give brightness in times of darkness .
May the leaves
Teach us how to grow again after a fall .
May the tree
Stand still till there's life on earth .
May the rain
Wash away all our worries .
May the breeze
Blow new strength into our being .
May the mountains
Take us to another high peaks .
May the clouds
Let us fly in this far spread sky .
May the universe
Design itself in a more beautiful way to give us shelter .
May the flowers
Make our lives more colourful .

May the wild
Teaches us peace .
May we walk
Gently through the world and, knows it's beauty the rest days of our life .
– Rishika Jain

ABOUT THE AUTHOR

Rishika Jain is a budding writer. She is currently doing her graduation in BPT.

Her aim is to become a doctor whose writeups can take people to an another world of words created by her. She is also a co-author of many published anthologies.

9. STORY OF INSPIRATION

I am stunning
OHK!
This is not a phrase
I learn from my pain
That inspire me to gain
The problems of my life
That freezes me like ice
The storm of obstacles
Made my path impossible
The days gone with sorrow
Nothing in my hand for tomorrow
My mind start depressing
My lines are distressing
I just give up
I lost up
everything vanishes
Then,
One day a ray of hope
And my thoughts climb a rope
Which makes me think
And my solution makes a link
But still INSPIRATION has to be reveal

Which revolve my wheel
And that's nothing
But NATURE
That taught me a lecture
Now, problem has a clear picture
And my mind makes a posture
The leaves of tree
taught me to be free
The waves in sea
taught my problems to flee
The open Sky
taught me to rise high
The flying birds
gives my dreams a Green Card
The fire of homa
taught me to remove negative Aroma
The pets around me
taught me to ignore strangers to be
And this endless nature
give me listen to learn
TO BE A INSPIRATION
of your own Nation
– Harshita Kunchhal

ABOUT THE AUTHOR

This is Harshita Kunchhal.

Love to words

Life to write

Brain to pen down

10. INSPIRATION (AN ACROSTIC POEM)

I- Initiate the idea,
N- Never lose the grip,
S- Start hoping,
P- Perform your best.
I- In difficulties,
R- Reinforce your strength.
A- Attain people's attention
T- Tear off the misconceptions.
I- Increase the level of difficulty for others in meeting your capabilities.
O- On the way of your life, set your journey as remarkable.
N- Never lose hope and always trust yourself.
– Niteesha Duvvuri

ABOUT THE AUTHOR

Niteesha is a passionate writer. She loves writing. She has started her writing journey in 2018. She wants to grow as a writer with more creative ideas. You can find her on Your quote app and on Instagram.

Thank You!

Thank you for choosing
"HEARTENING POEMS"

Printed by Libri Plureos GmbH in Hamburg,
Germany